Unadoptable Joy

A memoir in poetry and prose

J. L. Wright

ISBN: 10: 1974364925
ISBN-13: 978-1974364923

All art by J. L Wright and Katherine Smith

DEDICATION

For my wife, Katherine, my inspiration, guide, and guardian.

CONTENTS

ACKNOWLEDGMENTS

I would like to express my gratitude to the myriad people who saw me through this book and to those who inspired, supported, critiqued, and edited. My fellow writers in Bellingham, WA have been unbelievable in this process.

Support of me as a poet has also come from various media that have published several of these poems and others.

'Distress' published in *The Pain That Unites Us All - An Anthology*

'Crushed Quartz Concrete (Imaginings of a Child)' published in *A Feast for the Mind - GNU Journal*

'Hometown Hibbing, Minnesota' published in *Spring 2017 Peace Poems, Volume Two: A collection of poems by border poets from Canada and the United States.*

'She' published in *Heal(er) Magazine*

I. PREFACE:

I am holding onto a dream of a birth family.

I should have grown up in a home with two loving birth parents who cared for and supported their children like my foster parents. The home my parents gave me should have been in a nice neighborhood with good schools. My parents of origin shouldn't have fought in front of their kids. They shouldn't have gotten in trouble with the police. My brothers and sister, those related by blood, should have had an opportunity to get to know me, play with me, laugh with me, love me. I should have been close enough to them to judge them, or at least to judge them with the familiar knowledge that comes with siblinghood. I wanted them to be my true family.

Instead, I grew up in a great home with good parents who did their best. These were not my birth parents. My birth brother and foster sister played with me and got to know me enough that they could overlook and even celebrate my idiosyncrasies. We had a nice house in a great neighborhood with good schools where I thrived. Although my brother challenged the system, he did so not because of where he was but due to who he was. Our family history followed him and was his crutch and manacle.

Writing and telling the stories of my life lets me see things with 20/20 hindsight and, although my foster family wasn't perfect and I missed growing up with my biological sister, half-brother and parents, we all made it. But we didn't make it together.

The good thing about memoirs are they are just one person's reality. With time, many of my memories have faded and warped by stories told or made up. For me, many of my memories created are puzzle pieces that seemed to fit. For example, our family has a photograph of my siblings I grew up with and me standing near a Christmas wreath. All three children are neatly dressed but instead of smiles we wear somber expressions. At one point, I remember asking my foster mom where the photo was taken. She told me we were all at the dentist office. Now why would we have taken a family holiday photo at a dentist office? I have no clue - but that's what I remember.

I'm sure there are some memories that cannot be corroborated by any family member living or dead and some so fantastically altered by time and melded by imagination that my relatives would consider them merely conjecture. But the tales told here are based on my past and the lessons that I learned and the ways I have grown and changed. All representations are seen through the lens I was given. Different lenses would no doubt reveal different truths from life's different witnesses. My lens has changed and the stories are about me under a microscope and not those who - through relationships of birth or foster family - held me down or raised me up.

II. A CHILD LIES CRYING IN
CRIB UNHEARD

Closeted

Rubber boots, heavy black galoshes with brass
clasps, the kind real men wear, comfort me.
The smell of rubber, acrid like skunk musk,
in the dark tight room, I claim, soothes me.
Just off the living room of our public housing
apartment near the front door, I am closeted.

The front door I heard slam too many times as one
leaves. The door that when some stranger bangs is
even scarier. The people who knock take us away,
they separate us. I don't know if we will come back
to this place or another, if we will be "us" again.

This night the boots are cold and wet. His raincoat
drips on me. Familiar voices - loud even through my
hands over my ears. I look through the crack, by
the hinges and see him hit her,
open hand on her left cheek.

He stomps toward the closet, flings the door open,
grabs the raincoat, spins it around and on.

I press myself back against the wall.

He reaches down for the boots; his voice drops to
a whisper. He turns. One chubby worn finger points
at me. He glances at her over his shoulder, puts on
the boots, and clomps out. The door slams.

Broken

white Corelle® plate flies and crashes against a wall
gut wrenching pain from dry heaves rip flesh from rib cage
and another child lays on a cool tile floor face down
unemployed dad avoids overly friendly mom

gut wrenching pain from dry heaves rip flesh from rib cage
father mother sister brother people in a family
unemployed dad avoids overly friendly mom
counseling leads to hospitalization

father mother sister brother people in a family
pink duplex public housing on an elm lined street
counseling leads to hospitalization
oversized bathrobe and used pajamas are a present

pink duplex public housing on an elm lined street
grandparents, CPS, police try to improve the situation
oversized bathrobe and used pajamas are a present
coffee perks in the shiny silver electric pot on the counter

grandparents, CPS, police try to improve the situation
but a child lies crying in crib unheard
coffee perks in the shiny silver electric pot on the counter
not one, not two, but three children alone in the world

but a child lies crying in crib unheard
and another child lays on a cool tile floor face down
not one, not two, but three children alone in the world
white Corelle® plate flies and crashes against a wall

Impetigo Girl

Bullous blisters
tearing skin from flesh
Hands bandaged to stop scratching
Sit on them, don't rub yourself on the chair
Ointment on oozing and orange baby aspirin
Impetigo girl a seeping scab head to toe
Impetigo girl smelling of camphor
Impetigo girl can't sit by me
wash your hands and your
bedding she's
contagious

A Place I Didn't Want to Be

brown stucco building with arches
inviting impenetrable front doors
courtyard with thick stucco walls
inverted arches topped with iron bars
nearly overgrown with lilacs and trees
a state building, not for me

this is where we sang Jesus Loves Me
in first floor offices under arches
welcoming potential parents and family trees
plotting lives of children behind locked doors
families created or torn within these walls
ours broken completely by happy hour bars

office on the right behind the papered walls
housed the woman who guarded me
sitting stiffly on a wooden chair with bars
pursed lips and eyebrow arches
she carries the key for the front doors
made from thick solid oak trees

upstairs, small faces looked out on trees
from waiting rooms and office walls
counseling sessions behind shut doors
waiting to see who was here for me
unheard but able to hear, ear arches
concerns discussed they may be bars

wants for family, not chocolate bars
sister, brothers, uncle, family trees
crying convulsions, my body arches
through a lilac bush and over walls
my hero, my brother carried me
we left through the kitchen doors

scratched and scraped beyond unopened doors
until a station wagon with backseat bars
appears passenger door flies open for me
we enjoy the drive along the lane of trees
return behind the thick brown stucco walls
three strikes each on our small bare arches

appreciated architecture of arches and heavy doors
the walls and bars now inside my soul
trees outside are freedom for me

Enoch

To speak of it
cannot be done

The temple ravaged
by the god of son

Altar broken
baptismal too

No words spoken
'tween me and you

Desecrated
flower bloom

Apparition
trudges from tomb

A Letter

Dear   Mom
I know I'm not   even there yet
when I get there, it won't be all ice cream and
cupcakes – I may be shy or sassy, I may move
too fast or too slow – I may not like broccoli or
green beans or even football or games – I
will not say it when you need to hear it
most – so keep this card handy
because I love you already
Mom – your future
foster
child

III. LOOKING INTO THE GLASS

Crushed Quartz Concrete
(Imaginings of a Child)

twinkle twinkle sunny sidewalk
diamonds and gold under my feet
dandelion lemonade
playing house and hide and seek

the alley becomes the front lines
in the game of war as neighborhoods
get smaller while our town is explored
empty houses with haunted tales
call to rally for businesses failed
passion becomes political purpose
migrating teens to rural roads
the state comes into fervent focus
beyond the dream of leading
people, a country, the nation

light sabers lead the charge
to the moon made of cheese
and pony rides on daddy's knees

First Kiss

Deep in the depths of the second-grade cloak room, I attack Eric.

The honor patrol team would be ours the following year before he was to move away.

But now, I just wanted him to know I was in "like." In "like" with him, the second tallest boy with the close-cut hair, military style - not flat top, smooth bronze skin, and his haunting green eyes.

I hung up my coat, set my SCOOBY DOO ® lunch box on the shelf above, and called him over. We were the last two in the room. He said, "We have to hurry, the bell is going to ring."

I plead in a determined whisper, "Come here Eric, I need to tell you a secret."

Eric comes over and leans down as my curved finger instructs. He crooks his ear to my mouth so he can hear. I grab his head with both hands, push him against the adjacent wall, and push my moist mouth against part of his face; his cheek, I think, as I had my eyes closed. I release him as he pushes against my chest. I fall to the floor in a thud, landing on my bottom. He scrambles toward the door.

The doorway fills with the teacher who asks, "What is going on in here?"

"She kissed me," Eric states gruffly as he rubs his sleeved arm against his face and pushes pass the teacher.

I sat firmly on the floor and began pulling my boots off my feet to put on my shoes.

The teacher's hands rise to her hips. "Is that true, Joy, did you kiss him?"

"Yep," I reply.

"Put your shoes on, go to the principal's office, and tell him what happened."

"Yes, ma'am," I say with a smirk.

Strip Poker

A night without parents there
a game of cards becomes a way
determining what traits, we share.

Hidden by the clothes we wear
a child's question turned play
a night without parents there.

> Looking into the glass we stare
> thinking what would grownups say
> determining what traits we share.

> Faces and bodies not a pair
> one book says we came from clay
> a night without parents there.

> Questioning as we stand bare
> the kinship - second toe hairs
> determining what traits we share.

Related we are unaware
uncertain their hair turned gray.
A night without parents there,
determining what traits we share.

Dreams

I.   To dream the impossible

If it is imaginable it is doable.
I sat atop the swing set's main
cross beam about 20' in the air.
Ah, to be a gymnast like Olga
Korbut, before Nadia Comaneci.
I had aced the high jump, could
do anything on the monkey bars and
now wanted to practice the uneven
bars but I only had one.

> "How did you get up there?" Mrs. Dillon
> called. "Get down, no don't," her voice
> changed to fear.

I switched my position, wrapped one leg
over the bar and the other hung straight down.
Mr. D, the principal, and Mr.
Niemi, the fifth-grade teacher, were running
out in our direction.

> "Take the children inside," Mr. D. called to
> Mrs. Dillon.

> "Slide over to this pole," Mr. Niemi said in a
> purposeful tone as he grabbed one of the
> angled legs of the swing set.

"Watch this!" I responded. I leaned forward and
rotated over the bar. My body straight, I held tight.

A loud gasp from below.

"I knew I could do it!" I said as I walked myself sideways - hand to hand, toward the pole Mr. Niemi held. I wrapped my legs around it, completed my descent, and thought...

Next time a dismount!

II. Bedtime prayers and night-night kisses

If I should die, my soul to take,
shouldn't it be given
freely
willingly
openly
shared
not with a being from a book of
fables teaching life lessons
but with the universe needing
my positive energy?

III. Nightmares

The monster under my bed
frighteningly friendly
Sendakian creature,
long claws and teeth
faux fur body the texture of
my decorative pillow on my bed.
He drooled on my pillow when
I let him stay with me but he

also banged my head against
the wall or window beside my bed.
Dad would have to wake me to
get him to stop, yet, I didn't understand
why I was afraid to go to bed.

IV. And when I dream

My face relaxes cheeks
raise into a natural smile.

Not a smirk like childhood
school photos
artificial
full of fear.

Not just smizing eyes
or an evil smirk but a
peaceful "the undertaker did a great job" grin.

Hamlet:

"To sleep, perchance to dream—ay, there's the rub."

Shame buried

shame buried
in a large wooden toy box
in an unfinished basement
bathroom corner
hidden beneath
faded stuffed animals
button eyes missing
hot wheel tracks
deflated rubber balls
dolls stained red
by battery acid

learning the toys
were going to go
a dive in the box
found some shame
in adolescent understanding
but two stains remained
holes eaten through
cotton by womanhood
or just a girl not yet
prepared left here
not to be found but
to be forgotten

discovery day shame
raised its ugly
head and screamed
an understanding apology
from mother
to daughter
simultaneous tears
cleanse a battery of wormwood

Only the Good Die Young

I thought it might be me
migraines and menses
nine-year-old avid reader devours
Island of the Blue Dolphins,
Love Story, and
The Other Side of the Mountain
tragedy affects the heroine
her demise reflects

a purpose for life

my sins
oh, so few
do not make me worthy of the sword

Unlabeled

all in a name
to be the same
parents listed
my eyes misted
it wasn't Wright
it caused a fight
I ran away

What could I say?

Inner Self

Amongst the confusion
and terror
a small inner self exists
Colorful and vibrant
our self glows
from doubt to elation
from cornflower
to sweet pink -
a happy child's box of 64
used and explored

IV.   JOINING "OUR FAMILY"

September 9, 1971

Dear Social Worker:

It wasn't "Wright," the teacher called, "Campbell." I told her, "Wright." She thought I said "right" so she said "Campbell" the next day too. I ran to the bathroom and cried. My classmate came to ask if I was ok. I said, "no" and ran away. I walked through alleys and hid until I knew school was over and finally went home.

Mom was waiting, she knew what happened. She took me to school the next day. We met with the principal and teacher, both apologized but it was too late. The other kids knew I wasn't "Wright." Some knew I wasn't even right. I could write any name on my paper but it wouldn't be true. Those parents aren't my parents.

Is there anything you can do?

J. Campbell

October 19, 1971

Dear Mr. And Mrs. Wright:

I received and reviewed the letter your young ward, J sent. Although it's unusual, it could be possible that the child could change her last name to Wright. Unlike an adoption, she would still have access to her records as an adult.

Please contact the local courts to determine fees. The state will cover her legal fees, however any other costs will be your responsibility.

Respectfully,

Social Worker

November 15, 1971

Dear Judge of the Court:

I am a foster child who would like to change my name to my parents last name. The other kids at school tease me when they find out I don't have the same last name. Respectfully submitted,

J. Campbell

March 7, 1972

Dear Miss Campbell:

Your court date is scheduled for 8:30 am on Friday, April 7, 1972. This will be a closed court session. Please arrive ten minutes early to review documents.

County Court

April 7, 1972

Dear Teacher:

My name is now and will always be J. Wright. Please refer to me as such now and in the future.

Sincerely and thank you,

J. Wright

The Sofa

The charcoal gray nylon upholstery with silver shiny threads here and there covered the three-piece corner davenport. A true piece of furniture had been loved and respected for years since joining "our family" in the late fifties. It had traveled from our home in Minneapolis to our house in Chisholm and finally to Hibbing. Eventually, it moved back to Chisholm as a hand-me-down to my sister and her family.

By 1972, Mom had grown weary of her end where she smoked, drank coffee, and ate popcorn nightly. Her end where she had control of the front door; as she had the quickest access to it. And from which Mom informed Dad, the couch needed to change. For her, this meant something new, for Dad this meant something different.

The difference discovered after shopping at the two local furniture stores and deciding what couches they had was "overpriced crap"! With moms sewing skills and dad's carpentry skills and three children as menial labor, our family would take the couch apart, rebuild and recover it.

Mom was excited, she went shopping for fabric. The kids went with her, that might have been a poor choice as shag carpet was the norm in the design studios and Naugahyde and faux fur were the scene for upholstery. Since Naugahyde was unforgiving as a fabric to stretch around curves, faux fur was the choice. Mom wanted a dark color but not black she went with navy blue. The yardage and foam and binding and pillow fluff went home with the family and the work began.

The basement became an upholstery workroom. First the teardown. Seam rippers carefully running the edges of the rolled trim so patterns made and followed. Down to a skeleton of hard wood frame with metal brackets and springs. Small crowbars released the worn springs that needed tightening. Then sewing machine buzzing the new fabric took on known shapes and small fingers guiding a thin rope into mom's proficient hands. Staple gun attaching batting around each piece of wood and foam so they wouldn't rub through with time. Tack hammer gently easing the new fabric onto the battened frame while carefully untucking corners inside each cushion. Finally carrying each piece carefully back up the narrow steep basement stairs and sitting the davenport back in the original place along the walls. New matching throw pillows added. Our family project masterfully complete.

Mom assumed her position. The new rule, no eating on the sofa. As one of the neighbors came for a visit and admired our expert work she noted the fabric, not to her liking. It reminded her of something new on TV. A character on one of the television shows the kids watch on PBS. And then she said it! Our beautiful piece of furniture became known as the neighborhoods' Cookie Monster.

Hometown Hibbing, Minnesota

Elms eaten by army worms cut to stop the spread of disease
stolen pansies excavated and brought home to mother
fireworks celebrate freedom on the Fourth of July
drive-in movies cannot start until the sun is fully set

Stolen pansies excavated and brought home to mother
rust colored water hiding wreckage in emotionless depths
drive-in movies cannot start until the sun is fully set
our village is home to memories of innocence and safety

Rust colored water hiding wreckage in emotionless depths
childhood freedom in fleeting hot summer days
our village is home to memories of innocence and safety
red, white, and blue denim hip huggers on teeny boppers

Childhood freedom in fleeting hot summer days
unending crystal blue skies invite eventual escape
red, white, and blue denim hip huggers on teeny boppers
watermelon eaten outside by children with dripping chins

Unending crystal blue skies invite eventual escape
the nation secured in democracy is safe for today
watermelon eaten outside by children with dripping chins
Seina waters heritage roses in a housedress and slippers

The nation secured in democracy is safe for today
fireworks celebrate freedom on the Fourth of July
Seina waters heritage roses in a housedress and slipper
elms eaten by army worms cut to stop the spread of disease

Property of the State

Being a foster kid
is unforgettable
social workers visit often enough
so, we never could forget

Home checks
to ensure we were
fed, clothed, treated right
scheduled by phone or letter

Mom would tell me
Panic, were they going to take us away?
the early years, so chaotic
change always uncomfortable

Visits from social workers
often the predecessors of change
there had been other foster homes
our siblings torn from us
raised in different households
unseen yet unforgotten

White sedan, big letters,
"Child Welfare Department",
pulls up in front of the house,
checks the address on the brown file folder
drives around the block, parks down a few houses
very inconspicuous

Young put-together lady knocks on front door
and rings doorbell, yes both, always

anxiously I get mom, she taught us
not to open doors to strangers.

Mom tells us to let her in
as the door swings open,
Mom appears from the kitchen
Social Worker introduces herself
shake hands with the three of us.

living room or the kitchen?
coffee offered
discussion of grades, school
our free time, family outings
and our BEHAVIOR

honest Mom tells female stranger
I swear and roll my eyes
Mom's concern about my health
blanketed in shame, I must discuss details
about my cycle and bathroom habits
admonishment for masturbation

the social worker speaks to Mom alone
about expenses and budget
there is never enough money

then she speaks to us kids alone
our chance to tell on mom and dad
if we want

Have we been spanked?
this is against the rules
Did we want to continue living here?

we ask questions
about our real parents
about our siblings
we get no answers

visit over, mom walks social worker
back to car with final private comments,
waves at prying eyes of neighbors.
everyone knew We were foster kids

Hand Me Downs

The pink blouse
five pearl buttons on each cuff
wide collar
puffy sleeves
blue satin stitched capital letter
embroidered on the chest - a 'D'

I wore it under a sweater vest
so no one would see

But I knew

gym classes were B days
Tuesdays and Thursdays
but on weeks with no class on Monday
the schedule changed
I was found out
trying to slide the blouse off
over my head with sweater entangled
excuse, lie, story. . .   unreal

But I knew

the embroidery
lay heavy on my heart
like the lie that
the blouse was mine
my truth; I wasn't good enough,
pretty enough, skinny enough,
tall enough,
not kin enough . . .

But I knew

I just wanted the 'D' gone
I wanted to wear the blouse proudly,
it was sewn so beautifully
and such a pretty color
Mother deserved recognition
for all her hard work

the pink blouse hung in my closet
seeking reprieve
a day of sunshine and
mothball free air

if only it could be
actively appreciated
until the color began to fade
from washing

after long consideration,
it was time
donations of closet clearings
the blouse impeccably ironed
and nearly new
went into the black garbage bag
with the pants that were too short
and the sweater with a snag

But I knew

dropped off at the local Salvation Army
I wondered, should I have kept the pearl buttons
cut out and framed the beautiful 'D'

no further consideration
the closet space filled with another,
a navy-blue batwing blouse; fun and playful
it fit me better than 'D' as it was shorter
a date night go-to and looked great with jeans

during the second week
of the new school year,
everyone still minding what
others were wearing
I saw it, as I climbed the stairs
to second floor English

there she was
wearing the bright pink blouse
proudly with navy skirt and tights
she carried her books near her chest
she stepped toward me,
lowered her books.
"Hi Dawn," I said,
"I love your blouse!"

Distress

There is
  always
    someone
      suffering
        more than I.
Someone
  with unending
    pain.
Does that
  lighten my load
    or make me
      feel shame?
I want
  to know
    that MY burden
      is the heaviest,
      the saddest.
But even,
  in the moment
    I know
      it is not.
I cannot
  understand
    your pain,
      your burden,
        your loss.
We both
  suffer
    together
      alone.

Evolutionary

From a house of terror
where abuse abounded
I am from a drunk and a whore
sick, strung out, poor
survivors who let me go

Bequeathed with looks and build
from an unknown woman
a compassionate soul
I am from a dysfunctional family
without heritage from fear to
strength and endurance

Muffled voices in the other room
the smell of rubber boots
I am from unreal stories to wrap
my mind around to the security of
no security in seven foster homes
with cereal for supper

The art of language and daily schedules
develop me from Jesus Loves Me to
Amazing Grace from the projects to
suburbia knowing "intelligence will
carry me through" from relatives,
unwanted - separate differing lives
my past is me

Family Tree of Life

my family tree of life
has roots that run deep into dry dead
ground life giving rain once plentiful
no longer dancing across
the plains   leaves once green now
mostly lay scattered upon hardened

brown

clay,

curled,

rotting

yet the only

possibility for

continued   life

July Epiphany

Driving to work in my cool old car
I stopped at a light and waited
Before the changing - a honk and a wave and thumbs
up - next to me
Made me smile
I waved back and smiled even wider
I like the feel of it on my face
I thought about a picture of myself I saw the other
day, I was grinning open mouth, teeth showing
I have a nice smile I thought

Epiphany...I like to smile

It's been 10 years since my mom passed
I was getting kind of crazy before that with
the divorce and all the silliness of men
Got even crazier after that
Got crazy because I wanted to smile
I wanted to feel a beaming smile
I wanted a belly laugh to come out of me and fill a
room the way my mom's used to

This morning I felt the wind in my hair
and grinned ear to ear
I chuckled at the light hearing
the thump thump to the left of me
And the oom-pahs to my right
It wasn't a belly laugh yet but the day is still young

April 23rd

Why, on the one of the prettiest spring days with
the flower blooms swaying their scents my way,
should I remember, touching your hands;
to say goodbye, as you had already left?

Why on this day should I remember touching
your hand - still and cold on a day that you were
no longer you, in the box, where you still lie?

There I saw your yellowing finger nails, longer than
they should be; I thought, they still grow for a time.
I saw your veins green and raised, your age spots
darker than your freckles.

These were the hands which earned our level
of comfort. The hands I held tightly as I stood on
your feet to dance. The hands that built furniture for
my Barbie® and painted bedroom walls Pepto-
Bismol® pink.

The one which grabbed the steering wheel as I fell
asleep, the first time I drove. One rose when they
asked, "Who gives this woman?"

The hands that helped clear the yard of the first house
I rented. The hands I held as we prayed together, for
the last time, as the pastor gave you 'last rights.'

Why, on this day should I remember your hands so
clearly? On this sullen anniversary, I have no choice
but

to remember the hands that were never raised against me. The hands that wrapped me and comforted me.

These hands with warped knuckles from playing baseball without a glove; entertained me with piano tunes, kept me safe crossing busy streets, taught me to change a tire, and gave me love – with their gentle calloused touch.

Hour Glass

The sands of time drift
slowly across the deserts
of life - each grain moved
by the **wind** to its next
place **to lie. Each** grain
settles into a cradle
of sand grains
and waits for
another gust of wind
to move them slowly
toward new destinations.
Each of us like a grain of
sand is briefly cradled by our
family and friends until it is
time for us to move on.

I am who

I'm too old to be her
the beauty that dies the tragic death
in the tear jerker movie

I'm too old to be her
the cheerleader who grew up
to be a realtor always dressed for the sale

I'm her
  the girl with imagination, promise, and potential
  a person too smart and critical
  to be a decent friend

  a teacher with too much compassion
  and too many ideas

  a femme-fatal who accepts her gifts
  of a narrow waist and wide hips

  the wife who supports her partner
  completely in her dreams

I still have ambition to be her
  the woman who trades her love of others
  for her personal passion

  the lady who leads by exquisite example
  and mentors others

  The writer whose words
  influence positive change for the future

Mobius Strip

Life is a Mobius strip of time folding upon itself. To be here again 31 years between visits measured a lifetime from an un-mothered child to mothering adult.

I remember remembering. April 1997 and I had returned to Minnesota in a rush, no a frenzy because she, mom foster mom, was trying to follow Dad into the next life.

I drove my rental car insanely from the airport to the hospital, which looked vaguely familiar, and took the nearest elevator to ICU to see her. I got on the elevator. A nurse in mask and scrubs with the patient on the gurney rode with me. Safely on the 7th floor, I checked into the ICU waiting room and saw Debs and Terry right away. They both looked exhausted. Debs explained, surgery continued. Debs' eyes, more red than brown, were surrounded by gray and blue veins like a boxer after a bout. Terry, surprisingly thin, looked haggard as well from a long drive and a longer wait here in a room full of strangers.

They told me Mom was taken back into surgery because the abdominal aorta that had burst earlier in the week was indeed a predecessor to the triple bypass currently undertaken.

As we spoke, a candy striper came over to us, "The surgery is over and your mom will be in an ICU room shortly. One of the surgeons would like to speak with you."

A man in blue scrubs escorted us through the double swinging doors and into the Intensive Care Unit. Mom's room had a sliding glass door, which opened as we approached. A sheet lay across her, barely covering her torso. The room was freezing. A nurse came over from the other patient and introduced herself. She would be taking care of Mom: dayshift from 6 a.m. to 6 p.m.

The doctor walked over to Mom, took her hand, and patted it hard.

"Wake up Ruth," he said louder. "You have company."

She moaned and barely moved her head.

"Ruth! Ruth!," he nearly shouting as he slapped her hand with another thud.

Finally, she opened her eyes. She grimaced with pain and began to lift her hand towards her throat. The doctor stopped her hand as he introduced himself to her. "You have a tube in your throat, Ruth." He explained, "Of course it's going to hurt. Right now, pain is a good thing."

Mom dozed. Debs and Terry went to his sister's house for some sleep. Sleep had already become a precious commodity, which would be measured in quality, not quantity. In the days to come, this commodity became as essential as air.

I stayed awake and watched over our precious mother as much as the ICU would let me. I was allowed in her room 15 minutes of every hour. Then I'd return to the ICU waiting room and call relatives with updates.

After the first night, a candy striper approached with a cup of coffee, a pillow, and a blanket.

"You're welcome to sleep here, but the waiting

room on 4 East might be quieter," she told me.

Visitors had already begun milling into the ICU waiting room.

I took my blanket and pillow, abandoned the cup of coffee, and wandered towards the elevator. Finally, I noticed the bright red sign on the elevator doors: SURGICAL TEAMS ONLY. These were the elevators I had arrived here in.

I shuffled down the corridor around another corner and found the VISITORS elevator. I climbed aboard and looked at the buttons before me. Instead of pressing 4, I pressed L. Beside the L, a sign read LOBBY AND CHAPEL. I decided that was where I needed to be.

I entered the chapel and signed the guest book, which summoned me before I rounded a walnut wall separating the chapel from the hospital corridor. It was a small room with red carpet matching the cushions on the six pews. At the far end, an altar with a silver crucifix stood in front of a lighted stained-glass window. I sat in the back corner, soaked in the quietness of this place, and fell asleep holding the pillow and blanket in my lap.

I awoke to soft sobs of a man in the front of the chapel, kneeling before the altar. I collected myself to a wakeful state, gathered the blanket and pillow and slipped out quietly. I found the nearest handicap bathroom, so I had privacy to slip off my blouse to wash my face and underarms. I decided that I really needed to clean up, though. First, I had to return the pillow and blanket to the ICU waiting room. The VISITORS elevator brought me slowly up to the 7th floor. It stopped at every floor. People on - people off. I had no idea what time it was. The sign in sheet sat beside a small clock. 9:30 a.m., it read. I thought Day Two.

I must have slept for just over an hour. Still, I felt quite rested but grimy. Debs and Terry were returning from Mom's room. Debs looked better than yesterday, but Terry looked worse.

"How's Mom?" I called. Debs lower lip quivered. Terry responded, "She's awake now. On and off, anyway."

Debs hugged me and in my ear whispered, "She looks so small."

"Yeah," I sighed, "But so does Terry," I retorted, trying to change the mood. "What the hell happened to you?" I almost pushed my sister away. "Are you alright? It's not your heart, is it?"

"No, I've just been on a diet," Terry replied. "I've lost 75 pounds so far. I want to lose 50 more."

"Good for you," I quipped. "I'm going to go see Mom now. Are you guys going to hang around?"

"Yep," Debs replied. "We'll be here all day."

I left them in the waiting room corner and walked through the unit's double doors. My chest hurt. I swallowed hard. I felt tears well up inside as I approached Mom's room. I tried to choke them all back, but as soon as the sliding glass doors opened a tear spilled down my cheek. Mom was awake. She tried to talk. I told her it was ok; we'd have plenty of time after they got the tube out of her throat. I told her Bill sent her love and that we were ok - which was a lie - I talked about the kids at school and the weather. She drifted back into something like sleep. I could leave now.

I walked straight past the waiting room, took the elevator, and walked out to the parking lot.

Shit! What the hell kind of rental car do I have? What color is it?

I pulled the key from my pocket. The paper tag read "white Miata."

Oh yeah, that must be it, I thought as I spied a small two-door sports coupe.

Sure enough, my overnight bag lay on the front seat, my plane ticket perched on top, right out in the open.

God, I gotta get my act together.

I sat in the driver's seat for a few moments deciding it still wasn't time to cry. Grabbing my bag instead, I headed towards the bathroom I had previously used. I cleaned up, changed, and dropped my bag back into the trunk of the 'white Miata.' I decided I had better eat something. I headed down to the hospital cafeteria in the basement of the building. The food smells wafted down the hallway. My stomach turned over once. I hadn't eaten since the day before yesterday yet I couldn't face real food yet or maybe it was the real people I might see there. Anyway, I got back on the VISITORS elevator and went back to the 7th floor.

Debs and Terry had been back in to see Mom and reported the doctor had removed the tube from her throat. She couldn't speak much but had tried. They decided to take a break and head over to the Mall just down the street. They invited me along but I declined. I hadn't flown 1200 miles to go shopping, I thought.

I went in to visit with Mom. Mom was looking better at this point. She had some color to her face and although she was puffy from fluids she looked better than the drawn pale face I had seen before. She smiled and, "Joy," creaked out her throat as she greeted me. "Hi Mom. Wow, you're looking a lot better." She raised an eyebrow at me questioning my words. "Yes, you're looking much better," I reassured her. I told her again about Bill sending his love, the weather, and the kids at school, and informed her Debs and Terry had gone shopping.

The nurse came over and connected yet another IV to her arms that were blackened from previous needle sticks. I asked what she was giving her. The nurse explained the pain medication currently administered to Mom and how it was timed. And when I had exhausted my questions and my understanding, I allowed her to go back and check on the other patient in the room.

Mom slumped out of consciousness. She mumbled she was cold. I pulled her blanket up under her chin the best I could and sat beside her on the chair. Mom began to shiver hard. She awoke with a jerk.

"I'm soooo cold," she called out with a weak voice and blue lips.

I stood and looked at her. Almost instantly, my mom's body swelled, her skin reddened, and her body shook.

"Nurse. My mom needs you," I called feeling a little shaky myself.

"I'll be there in just a moment," she responded.

My mother's body shook the entire bed as she seized. "Nurse, my mom needs you NOW!" I called louder.

"Just a moment," she responded calmly.

I walked towards the other patient's bed, tugged the curtain separating me from the nurse and her current patient. It slipped open loudly, metal wheels against metal track. "My mom is having an allergic reaction," I said.

The nurse pulled back the curtain so she could see Mom and in the same breath said. "She can't be; we're not giving her anything…" Her eyes widened as she rushed towards Mom.

Her heart rate was 210. The blipping machine echoed in my head. The nurse pressed a large red button and 5 different nurses flooded into the room. They asked me to leave.

"No," I said, as I eased my way to a corner of the room near the sliding glass door.

"Then stay out of the way," one male nurse demanded.

"Just save my mom," I demanded back at him.

The regular nurse was on her cell phone to Mom's doctor.

On the far wall of the room, in large print, **23**, with the word April below it hit my eyes and pierced my brain.

"You can't die today Mom!" I muttered, "It's Dad's day. You can't have it!"

Her nurse reported the allergic reaction to the doctor. Mom stabilized before a doctor arrived from dialysis. The attending nurse told the doctor that I was the one who recognized it as an allergic reaction.

He patted my arm, "Your mom's lucky to have a daughter like you."

I decided I needed to get away. Debs and Terry were back with bags from the Harley-Davidson Shop, Dunkin' Donuts, and Radio Shack. They offered me a donut, which I allowed to melt in my mouth as I relayed the events of the ICU room.

I went down to my Miata and got in and tried to remember how to drive it. I wasn't used to a 5 speed or the deep bucket seat since my daily driver was a '64 Beetle.

How glad I was that Hertz had given my Escort to someone else, and I would just have to suffer using the Miata until they could come and exchange cars.

I left the parking lot, heading north, not sure where I was or where I was going. It had been years since I had really driven around the Minneapolis area. I drove down the boulevard through a grove of elms and noticed a sign saying, Minnehaha Falls. Yes, I want to be near the water. Maybe near the water, I could cry. I turned into the first driveway. It was a cemetery.

What a wonderful quiet place and appropriate for today of all days.

Parking as close to the river as I could, I pulled a small notebook and pen from my bag. I walked to the water's edge and listened as the stream moved rapidly over rocks making it sing a sweet calling tune. I stepped out to a small island in the stream and sat on a large rock and began to talk to Dad.

It's 10 years now since you passed. Do you want Mom with you now? Did Mom realize it's your anniversary today? Is she tired and ready to go home? I miss you daddy. I wish you were here. I wouldn't feel quite so all-alone.

I tried to cry. Instead, my pen etched across the paper…

Beauty Never Dies

Beauty lies in green grass and blue skies,
quiet walks and dragonflies,
in special friends and baby cries,
babbling brooks and blueberry pies.

Beauty lies in soft summer winds
and butterflies,
in moms and dads and kids first tries.

Beauty comes from God on high.
Even when we ask why,
beauty never dies.

The tears came easily now. They flowed down my cheeks and arms and joined the stream. The babbling brook cushioned me into being where I was, and I could handle it.

Back at the hospital, the visits with Mom throughout Day Three became more productive as the healing processes strengthened her. My Miata was my comfort, my home away from home, my rescue from the hospital and my via into my heart and soul as I sped around the city on breaks from visits.

Day Four I decided to go all the way back to visit my past. I drove to the neighborhood where I first lived with this mother.

Ruth, Edward, and my sister Debra all lived quietly at 6525 Standish AV in Richfield MN. My brother Michael and I became part of the family with the assistance of The State of Minnesota's Department of Child Welfare. We moved into the house on Standish Avenue. It was the perfect home with an above ground pool, dollhouse, and park right next door. The small quiet neighborhood was on a strip of property adjacent to the airport and separate from the rest of the city limits of Richfield.

As I drove across the 66th ST bridge I noticed everything seemed wrong since the last time I had driven past this property.

The first avenue had several houses still standing quite normally but between and beyond especially as I neared Standish AV the landscape changed dramatically. Street upon street bore out the emptiness of the scene from a sci-fi movie. All the houses were gone. The street lamps stood in their posts and as twilight was approaching came on like you would expect them to. Fences lined property lines between lots, and driveways led into yards. But the houses were all gone. The airport had finally gotten them I realized. Even when we left the neighborhood, the airport had put a bid on our house because they wanted the surrounding land to expand one of their runways. The scene made me think, as a child, what I had imagined an atomic blast might do. I pulled into our driveway and parked. I shut off the engine and radio, opened the window, and leaned the seat back. I listened to the airplanes fly overhead and smelled the lilac bush in bloom and fell asleep. I slept like I had in the home which once stood here, safe and comfortable.

The next morning, I awoke with drool sticking to my cheek and hair. I used the cold coffee in my cup to wipe my face with a napkin from a fast food place I had stopped at the night before. I headed back to the hospital. Mom was getting out of ICU today, if all was well.

I found Mom sitting up in bed and telling two orderlies as they wheeled her past the waiting room doorway, "Don't drive so fast."

Mom was feeling better. After they parked her in her room, she sent me back down to ICU to get all the names of the nurses down there, so she could do something nice for them. She was still closely monitored, but this end of the hall was a regular hospital.

Mom and I chatted. She'd called her house. Everything was taken care of by her niece. I joked with her about using the bypass as a way of getting me to come home and visit. I would stay until she was out of the hospital. We talked about the family. Yes, I had gotten word to Michael about Mom's condition, but they were not letting him out to visit. I might drive over to Stillwater State Prison to see him since I was here, but she was my priority. The surgeon whom I had met before seeing Mom appeared. He looked much younger this time and had a softness about him, which he had not displayed in our previous meeting.

"Well, Ruth," he chimed, "when do you want to go home?"

"I don't think I'm ready for that yet Doc, but I do want to get out of this bed and start peeing in a toilet instead of a tube."

The doctor lifted the sheet which covered her. "Hell, I thought we got rid of that thing yesterday. Of course, you do Ruth." He asked if I wanted to stay while he checked her incisions.

"I've got no problem with that," I replied.

Mom looked away. I looked on as the doctor examined her chest and legs. He lifted her arms until she reported pain.

"I don't see any reason to keep you here longer than you need to be Ruth," he said.

"I'm going to get some food, Mom. I'll be back in a little bit."

Debs and Terry were getting off the elevator as I was getting on. I called Mom's new room number to them as the doors closed. I went down to the cafeteria and caught myself humming in the corridor before I approached the doors. My meal hit the bottom of my stomach like a rock but it felt good. It held me down to the chair so I could look around and see all the normal people enjoying their normal lunches on a normal day.

Back upstairs, Debs and Terry said goodbye. They were heading home to Hibbing since Mom was out of ICU. They had a teenager still at home to take care of or at least chase off to school every now and then. I hugged them both and said goodbyes.

That afternoon Mom received her first meal. Water, milk, tea, juice, broth, and Jell-O. Yum-yum. At nearly 4 o'clock, the physical therapist arrived with a wheelchair. She helped Mom gingerly into the chair, which took every ounce of strength Mom had. We went directly to the therapy room without the tour. We looked at menus, equipment, lists of exercises and no-nos. The therapist began wheeling Mom back to the room and asked if she was up for the grand tour. She replied that she was, so we cruised through the hallways of 7 East towards the nurses' station. As we rounded the high counter the therapist stopped to talk to the nurses and ask for some assistance to get Mom back into bed. I, on the other hand, stopped in my tracks by what I saw: a glass wall just across from the nurses' station.

"Mom, that was my room, wasn't it?" I asked.

"What floor are we on?" She asked back.

"Seven," I answered.

"Yeah, I guess that is it. How do you remember that? You were so little."

"I remember you, Momma. I remember crying because you left me here all alone."

"I had to baby," she said. "You had to have the surgery for your eyes."

"I know," a tear ran down my cheek.

The physical therapist asked what was wrong.

Mom explained, "Joy was the first child who had undergone corrective eye surgery here in 1966, and that room had been hers." She went on, "I didn't want to leave her here, but I had to. I had one child at home, and Joy's brother Michael was across town in another hospital with a broken collar bone. She was in a crib in that room. She started crying and asking where I was going. I pointed out the window to my car and told her she could wave at me. When I arrived home the babysitter was on the phone with the nursing staff here. Joy had tried to climb out the window to follow me home. The nurses wanted permission to put a net over the crib to keep her inside just in case she tried that one again."

A tear rolled down Mom's cheek.

We stood still for a moment, remembering.

I returned to Texas when Mom was moved to a rehab facility. She recovered from her bypass surgery yet joined dad later. Throughout my years since, I have never wondered where I will be 5 years from now or 10. I know I am in the right place. The place where, being me, I can be the most productive. I also know that I will revisit the places I've been before because life is a Mobius strip.

She

Strength and assurance
proud and strong
her resolve apparent

But trepidation is at the door
of excitement
She moves on

A glance over her shoulder
a longing sadness
only captures her for a moment

She calls forth her source
calls anger her sword
as her journey continues

V. QUESTIONS UNANSWERED

Finding my mother
I always knew it
would happen,
eventually. I would
find my mother. I had no
idea it would happen quite
the way it did. I had searched
for years. Called all the names I knew.
I wrote letters to strangers in the phone
book. I asked for information and then
decided why not Facebook. I searched for
names I knew. I found a few. Searched their
photos and found a familiar face, one I had
seen before. My mother in high school, in a
photo shown to me before by a biological
relative. Then I saw the picture of a white
vase. I slid the mouse and clicked on the
next picture, an older version of my
mother, hugging her Robert, my
uncle." I found my mother!"
My voice squeaked, "I found
my mother on Facebook."
I began to choke up,
finished my thought.
"She's dead," I realized.
The white vase was my mother's urn.

She's with you even when you don't want her to be and
      yet it makes you   want it even   more   her
ashes,   her   family,   her name. Not having
          roots Makes   me just a tree
               that's been
               fallen
               by the
               wind of
               a storm,
               tested and
             pulled from the
            ground. Was the soil
      not   strong enough? Was   there too much
sand and rain? Did the   other   trees   feel the ravages
of   the storm?   Were they there   to
    be my   protectors?   I have
        no forest   in which   to grow,
          and off   to the lumber
             yard we
             go.

biological parents

birth father

Quiet and reserved on his death bed - I met him.
I know this wasn't really him - just a ghost of a
former self. He didn't really want to meet me but his
girlfriend knew I wanted to meet him

Willing to answer questions, he didn't have much to
say: "You look like her." "I wasn't a nice guy."
"Divorce cured me of marriage," but confessed he
wasn't certain he divorced. (Maybe just an excuse to
not remarry) He admitted alcohol had taken his life,
his girlfriend had resurrected him.

This was our only chat, an hour passed, he tired,
needed to rest, it was our one meeting before he
departed this world.

I didn't get all my questions
answered so I imagined more...
  He was the long lost relative of the
  Campbell(R) soup company, he would quit a hard
job by just not showing up.
  He preferred fishing to hunting, was a war hero
because he was injured in a truck accident while
serving, his own fault.
  His favorite thing to do would be watching TV.
(at least I can blame my bad habit on someone)

birth mother

She took no opportunity offered to defend herself.
My sister tracked her down earlier but mom didn't
respond. Displeased, I continued looking. When I
found her (ashes in an urn) on Facebook, I reached
out to her brother, my uncle.

Like his sister, he was resistive. He said she had
reached out to him a few years earlier; after a fall, a
broken a hip,
no longer able to work,
at McDonalds.
He, her brother, tried to help
paid her rent, for a mobile home,
where she lived as a hoarder.

No other information provided.
No more contact accepted.

I imagine she was lonely,
felt guilty about her life choices,
worked hard, when she could,
appreciated her alone time,
until she didn't. (like me)

I've had to imagine what kind of parents
these people might have been
but I can't - as I can barely imagine
what kind of people these parents were.

Poetic Truth

In turbulent times,
we search for truth;
often elusive,
clouded by
chattering channels
of swelling
contradiction.
With leaves of wisdom
and blossoms of
knowledge inherited,
we cling to our roots.
A source of truth speaks.
Truth is an expansion
of facts, we inherit
in backward wisdom;
understanding experiences
in a reality now silenced.
Here we find a truth;
lived, personal, and specific.
We comprehend
empathy and compassion.

Inspired by Why Poetry Matters Now More Than Ever by Richard
Hammond 9/21/2016

VI. PROLOGUE

Writing Awe

Do words grey and weather like an old
barn board, an open-door policy
or the open-air roof?

Do they run along a ridge, as three warrior ghosts
wondering if they should go down the steep
embankment to help the fallen or join them in death?

Will words break free like the land being
pounded together and pulled
apart by westward expansion?

Are words shaken not stirred, granite
slurry compressed into blue streaked
glaciers crawling toward the sea?

Can my words last long enough to be looked
upon with awe? Would it be too much to ask
that they are spoken out loud?

Are these words too sad to read in public
because a private tear would tear them from
your heart like they were birthed from mine?

Will anyone care or applaud the effort,
understand the confluence of time and
energy in creation or contemplation?

Does considering where and why
- knowing it doesn't matter -
seem empty and meaningless?

This is for my future and yours
from your past and mine;
these words are worthy of awe.

ABOUT THE AUTHOR

J. L. Wright was born in 1962 in Minneapolis, Minnesota and grew up in seven different foster homes with and without her siblings. Without the possibility of adoption, she landed in a permanent foster home with one of her brothers.

J. L. did well in school and was the first in her family to attend college, where she earned a B.S from Bemidji State University and M.Ed. from University of Texas, Arlington. She is a certified educator who has touched the lives of students from age three to adult before leaving the classroom to become a fulltime RVer and author.

Writing since childhood, *Unadoptable Joy: A memoir in poetry and prose,* is her first book. J. L. explores life in her original voice and variety of writing styles. Recent publications include Heal(er), GNU Journal, Whatcom Watch, Solstice Magazine, and Peace Poets Anthology and Chapbook.

More about the experience of being a full-time RVer with her wife and dog can be found at A Reason, A Season, A Lifetime: Quitting our jobs, selling everything, and hitting the road.
http://newbiefulltimervers.blogspot.com/

79445642R00046

Made in the USA
Lexington, KY
22 January 2018